DR. LYNN RICHARDSON

SYMPH*ONY* *The*

A Guide to *Creating & Balancing*
MULTIPLE STREAM

Cover Design:
Electric Heart Media

Contributor:
Ingrid LaVon Woolfolk

Editors:
Kaylah Jones and Cydney Richardson

This book is dedicated to every person who can't sleep, who can't sit still, who can't quit even when you want to . . . keep grinding & keep the faith.

Build your empire one dollar at a time, one day at a time, and one income stream at a time.
Lynn Richardson

More Books By Lynn Richardson

Living Check to Monday: The Real Deal About Money, Credit and Financial Security

Living Beyond Check to Monday: A Spiritual Path to Wealth and Prosperity

Yes, You're Approved! The Real Deal About Getting a Mortgage and Buying a Home

Your Man & Your Money: How to Get'em and How to Keep'em

Put On Your Financial Armor: End Your Battle With Money for Good

Lynnergy: Lynnisms and Other Powerful Thoughts for Life and Business Success

Estate Planning Made Simple: Building Your Financial Brand Starts with Having a Plan!

Table of Contents

Foreword

Throughout my career, I've found it important to be aligned with the right people who care enough about me, my vision, and my business to help me help others. It's impossible to do this alone. All of the greats have a team of people helping them get to the next level. After being around influential people for a lifetime, I thought I had met them all. I was mistaken. Not only has Lynn Richardson helped me transform my business and build my financial empire faster than the speed of light, but she planted generational seeds that transformed my life.

"The Symphony: A Guide to Creating and Balancing Multiple Streams of Income" is not just a book, it has been my life. Since we started working together, my career morphed into an empire full of income streams I'd only dreamed of prior to meeting

Lynn Richardson. I went from being a rapper, DJ, and voiceover talent to the CEO of an entertainment firm and production company, writer and producer of tv/film, bonafide actor, philanthropist, book publisher, author, and so much more.

We have influenced women and men in entertainment, corporate America, and the nonprofit sector, as well as millennials, baby boomers and people in all stages of life! Careers have exploded. Relationships have expanded. Financial plans have been actualized and dreams have become reality. I hope you use this toolbox of information and take it back to your family and community so we can build wealth together, and ultimately, so we can change the world together.

MC Lyte
CEO, Sunni Gyrl Inc
Chairman, Hip Hop Sisters Foundation
Rapper, Actor, DJ, Voiceover Talent, Host
Music Supervisor, Producer/Director, Philanthropist

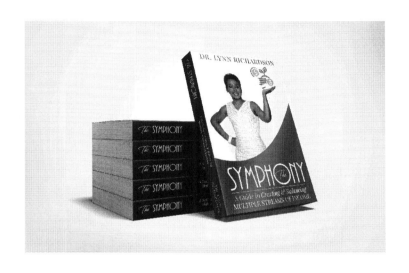

Introduction

My first memory of my existence is me being busy . . . my family and friends actually said I was "bossy," but I prefer the former term. I was ALWAYS busy. Busy doing what? Anything! Talking, creating, advising, organizing, arguing (LOL), researching, reasoning, reading, writing, exploring . . . yes indeed, I was always busy. I remember organizing the skating trips for the pre-teens I grew up with in the projects. Organizing those trips, planning the cheerleading competitions, debating whose turn it was to jump in the rope when we played double dutch, transferring myself (and my four year old little brother) to another school when I was 11 years old, and selling candy (and giving some of it away to my friends☹) in my grandfather's candy store located in the back pantry of his 4 bedroom brick abode in the projects of Chicago – all of that BUSYNESS prepared me for BUSINESS. I was a budding entrepreneur and I didn't even realize it. I was on my way to becoming a serial entrepreneur like many of the people I work with and admire today. There should probably be some kind of law against people like us. When we come up with an idea – when there is an opportunity to make money doing something we enjoy (or doing something we think we enjoy until we find out we don't!), to create something that makes money, or to join others who are making money – then we start a business!

In my early 20s, I was a jack of all trades and I mastered a few. Ok, let me tell the truth: I mastered NONE. If you came to my house on a Saturday, I could do your hair AND I could do your nails. I could help you with your financial aid because I was a financial aid counselor at a local college. I could write an insurance policy because I had an insurance license too. I could teach you how to quit your man or your woman, how to get a new job or two or three, how to write the perfect resume that would get you the coveted interview and I could even fix your image and your communication skills long enough to make sure you got the job (keeping it would be YOUR issue)! I was doing it all and I was so frustrated because my money did not match my effort. One minute I was happy with my new venture and the next I was overwhelmed and underpaid. It seemed as if I was doing everything and nothing.

This is where the SYMPHONY comes in. You see, the SYMPHONY is the place where you're operating in harmony. If you go to the orchestra, there are many different instruments and when played at the right time in the right key, they make one beautiful sound: a SYMPHONY. If your many businesses are operating in harmony – if you start the right business at the right time, then add an accompanying business or opportunity – then your business SYMPHONY will produce income streams that you can depend on for life.

The musical SYMPHONY has INSTRU-MENTS. The business SYMPHONY has INCOME-MENTS (it rhymes with and sounds like INSTRU-MENTS). Say it again to yourself: *INCOME-MENTS*. INSTRU-MENTS are devices that make sounds. INCOME-MENTS are businesses that make money.

INSTRU-MENTS must be handled with care. They must be cleaned, maintained, repaired, and stored properly. They must be studied by the user and the user must know every part of the INSTRU-MENT and which keys to play in order to master it and get the best sound out of it. The INSTRU-MENT is best when it's handled by someone who has been trained to play it well, who naturally plays it well, and/or who practices playing it regularly. When all of the INSTRU-MENTS in the orchestra meet these criteria, a musical SYMPHONY exists.

INCOME-MENTS must also be handled with care. They must be carefully planned, maintained, budgeted and managed properly. They must be studied by the owner and the owner must know every part of the INCOME-MENT and which elements to monetize in order to create demand and get the best stream of income out of it. The INCOME-MENT is best worked by someone who has been trained to execute it well, who naturally executes it well, and/or who practices executing and improving it regularly. When all of the INCOME-MENTS in your plan meet these criteria, a business SYMPHONY exists.

Get it? Over the next several chapters, you will:

1. Get trained on the basic elements of how businesses are treated in the American financial system and why it makes dollars *and* sense to have several of them.

2. Identify the gifts you naturally possess, the experiences you've encountered, and the skills you can enhance in order to create more INCOME-MENTS.

3. Identify the characteristics that will increase your discipline so you can pass your INCOME-MENTS on to future generations or sell them for a major profit.

Doesn't that sound like music to your money ears??

Okay . . . Let's work!

One Stream of Income
is Hazardous to Your Wealth!

Why do you need multiple streams of income? It's simple: if your job ends because technology replaces you, you're done. If the cost of goods in your business skyrockets, then you can't earn a profit. If your boss doesn't like you, then you will need to find another job or you may have to live in hell everyday. In other words, when you only have one stream of income, there is a high potential for your money to act funny and your change to act strange. If you only have one stream of income, there's a strong likelihood that you are either living check to check, or even worse, **Living Check to Monday** (that's when you get paid on Friday and you're broke on Monday, a beast tamed in my first book)!

When money is scarce, it can feel like the wilderness. It is. It's called the financial wilderness.

When you're in the wilderness, you may feel ashamed, alone, and most importantly, afraid. But let me tell you this: you are not alone, you can't do anything productive with fear, and there is NOTHING to be ashamed of. **NEWSFLASH**: everyone has either had a money problem, is having a money problem, or will have a money problem at some point in the future, so this isn't unique to you. This is not the time to beat up on yourself. This is not the time to go into a depression. I once heard Joyce Meyer say, *"Your behavior in the wilderness determines how long you stay there."* Ouch and Amen! She's right. In the Bible, the children of Israel were destined to enter the Promised Land, but because of their behavior in the wilderness, what started out as a very short trip turned into a 40-year journey, where those who failed to operate in faith and obedience never got to see the Promised Land. Don't let this be you. Don't stay stuck. It's time to create a plan and get your INCOME-MENTS working for you.

In order to get out of the financial wilderness, you must (1) **spend less money** (live by the 10-10-30-50 as discussed in my book **Living Check to Monday**), (2) **get more money** (aim for nine income streams with at least four of them being passive income streams; I will explain this later) and (3) **get your money back**. In this book, we're essentially dealing with (2) and (3). First, let's talk about why you need to get more money and how you're going to make it happen.

There are two systems in America, one for employees and one for businesses, and this is how the employee system works: If you are an employee and you make $50,000 a year, for example, the SYSTEM (IRS, state taxing authorities, FICA, etc) will take $15,000 or more right off the top. Yep. You'll have approximately

$35,000 left over and with that whopping $35,000, you are supposed to pay for all of your living expenses: rent, mortgage, car, travel, entertainment, mobile phones, tuition, daycare for your kids, kid's activities, etc. After you pay for everything you need, there's probably no money left, so you end up going into debt and robbing Peter to pay Paul while trying to figure out how to make ends meet. On top of that, at the end of the year, you get taxed on the whole $50,000 that you never even received!

This doesn't seem fair!

Uhmmm, guess what! **It's not fair!** The average American only gets about eight tax deductions (real estate taxes, mortgage interest, charitable donations, and a few others). But if you're an entrepreneur (**everyone's an entrepreneur**) with a homebased business, and you actually run your business like a business instead of a hobby (see the IRS explanation about whether your activity is a hobby versus a business in the resource section), there are over 475 tax deductions available for itemization on Schedule C of your 1040 tax return.

So if you find yourself in the first system, struggling to survive while paying more taxes than you should, don't fret, because there's another system for businesses. What kind of business? ANY business. Your sole proprietorship / homebased business in your home office, basement, loft, living room or attic. Microsoft. Your hair business. Walmart. Your resume writing business. CVS. Your consulting business. Here's the point I'm trying to make: you are in the same category with all of those big businesses. It doesn't matter what kind of business you own, but please understand that ALL businesses operate under the second system and this is how it works: if you have a homebased business and you make $50,000, first you get to deduct car expenses when you drive for business (interest, registration, oil changes, insurance, or mileage), mobile phones, internet, cable, meals with your business partners when you are conducting business, vacations (as long as you do a certain amount of business) and well over 475 other deductions that you probably have never heard of! Now let's compare this scenario to the employee example: if you make $50,000 and you own a business, and all of your documentable and legitimate business expenses (car, gas, mobile phones, internet, employees, business trips, business meals, etc) add up to $40,000, then you get to deduct the $40,000 in expenses from the $50,000 and pay taxes on the $10,000 that's left over!

This is how you **get your money back**!

Two Systems	Employee System	Business System
Income	$50,000	$50,000
Business Expenses to report on Schedule C of your 1040 Tax Return **FROM YOUR SOLE PROPRIETORSHIP OR HOME BASED BUSINESS**	- 0	-40,000
Taxable Income	$50,000	$10,000
Taxes Owed Based on 2019 - 2020 Tax Rates	$3,572 plus 32.5c for each dollar over $37,000 – **YOU OWE $7792**	**YOU OWE** **ZERO!**

If this is hard to believe, then don't just take my word for it, you can learn from my mentor, former IRS Attorney and CPA, Sandy Botkin. (Sign up for the free webinar and learn how you can get his free book: **7 Simple Ways to Legally Avoid Paying Taxes** www.taxbot.com/lynnrichardson). He once worked for the IRS and trained the auditors, but he left many years ago and now, all he does is train people like you and I:

people who once struggled but no longer have to struggle if we obtain and apply the tax knowledge he teaches. So whenever you spend money, you need to ask yourself this question: *"Can I legally and ethically document this as a business expense and **get my money back** when it's time to calculate what I have to pay the IRS?"* The more you answer "yes" to that question, the more money you will have in your pocket, and the more you will be motivated to run your business like a business (and not a hobby) and hopefully, you will be even more motivated now to create multiple streams of income and live by my mantra: ***it's always business* and everyone's an entrepreneur!**

I'm reminded of the virtuous woman of Proverbs because many people don't know that she was more than a great wife and woman of beauty and faith, but she was a great businesswoman. A review of the 31st chapter of the Book of Proverbs in the Bible reveals that she had at least nine jobs (my interpretation is she was a seamstress, a real estate professional, a distributor/trader at the merchant ships, teacher, vineyard owner, minister, household manager, philanthropist, and wife) . . . she had multiple streams of income indeed and yes, she was an entrepreneur! She managed her household and prepared meals for her servants before they woke up, which leads me to believe she was a great servant leader even in her household business affairs. She was seamstress and I imagine she sold her items retail to her neighbors, but she also went to the merchant ships to trade, sell larger quantities at wholesale prices, and get materials for future garments at a discount. She bought a piece of land and with her profit she planted a vineyard, doing so vigorously and ensuring that her trading was profitable. We should take her lead today as we battle the economy and we should minimize our financial setbacks and maximize our legacies by developing an entrepreneurial mindset. It's quite simple: being an entrepreneur with multiple streams of income, including a homebased business, is the key to determining whether or not you will be able to **get more money** and survive any potential economic setback and **get your money back** when tax season arrives.

One of my clients organizes her college reunion every year. Between site visits, travel, and meals, she spends over $6,000 each year and she's never made a profit in the past. Now that she is in business for herself as an Event Planning Consultant, she is able to write off every single dollar of her class reunion expense that is related to her homebased business as an Event Planning Consultant. (See IRS Publications 334 and 463)

What about this: have you ever invited business partners to your home to eat? Well, if you are an entrepreneur with at least one homebased business, and you truly have the intention to discuss business, then your gathering could be a business dinner! Place information about your business near the food. Take pictures of people looking at your business cards. Answer questions about your business and always ask for referrals. When guests ring your doorbell, greet them by saying *"How's business?"* Get it? I know you do! They may think you're strange, but who cares, you need to **get your money back**! As far as I'm concerned, *it's always business*, and what's most important, you can deduct what you spent on meals, invitations, and other items related to your business dinner on Schedule C of your 1040 tax return (the IRS no longer allow deductions for expenses associated with entertainment, so please be mindful that you must participate in entertainment activities SEPARATE from the meal if you want to deduct the cost of the meal).

And yes . . . *it's always business* when it comes to the kids too. I think EVERYONE should get paid to be a parent, grandparent, aunt, uncle, or God-parent! You spend thousands of dollars on the children in your life (activities, tuition, lunch money, vacations, etc). Money you can NEVER get back. But if you hire your children to work in your homebased business, you can pay each child a salary, deduct the salary as a business expense, **get your money back** when it's tax time (that's like getting paid, right?), then the child can use the money he/she earned to buy the things you were going to pay for anyway (tuition, activities, vacations, dance lessons, football camp, school clothes and supplies, etc etc). It's all tax free to the child and the parent (in a sole proprietorship / homebased business or in a partnership between the child's two parents) up to the first $12,000 per child! For me, $12,000 times three children equals $36,000 in additional tax write-offs each year. THAT'S A LOT OF MONEY! And when nieces and nephews and God-children ask me for money, I hire them to complete a project in one of my homebased businesses, I send them a 1099 at the end of the year and I write that off too! (See IRS Publications 15 and 535) In order to help the children offset any money they may owe to the IRS on the income they earn (if it's over $12,000 in a year), I encourage you to set up a sole proprietorship / homebased business for each child so they can write off their business expenses as well. I told you, in my circle, *it's always business* **and everyone's an entrepreneur!**

How To Hire Your Child To Work In Your Homebased Business:

1. Prepare a Job Description: There are dozens of jobs for older children (filing, household chores, helping at events, social media, bookkeeping, graphic design, technical support on devices, customer service) and here are a few for babies and toddlers: (1) a model in still photos promoting your business (business cards, website, pamphlets, etc.) (2) a talent in a video commercial for your business.

2. Send an Offer Letter.

3. Establish Payroll (transfer money from your business account to the child's bank account).

4. Conduct Performance Reviews.

Read the Section on Family Employees in IRS Publication 15

Read 5 Reasons to Hire Your Child at <u>www.sba.gov</u>
https://www.sba.gov/blogs/5-reasons-hire-your-child)

Let the INCOME-MENTS Begin!

Now that you know why it makes dollars AND sense to have a homebased business / sole proprietorship, it's time to start your business . . . NOW. So, if you haven't done so already, take a look at what you like to do, what you are good at, what people frequently complement you on, and/or what you previously considered a hobby and add these INCOME-MENTS (businesses that make money) to your business symphony. It doesn't matter if you're a motivational speaker, a hair stylist, or a direct sales agent for a multilevel marketing company. Here's an idea: everybody can be a consultant doing something they are knowledgeable in executing. Are you in education? You're an educational consultant for a new charter school or a tutoring / test preparation consultant. Are you a hair, makeup or wardrobe stylist? You're an image consultant. Do you enjoy helping others plan events? You're an event planning consultant. Do you clean homes for a living? You're a home management consultant to the many working women like me who need help keeping their households and their children in order (my children are grown and in college, but one came back home and brought her God-sister with her, so I'm *still* dealing with this, and as a result, I have a mean chores checklist available in the Resource section for any parent who needs it)!

To start your sole proprietorship / homebased business for less than $100, get some business cards, a website, phone number and email address using your name (For example: www.lynnrichardson.com dreamscometrue@lynnrichardson.com 888.LYNN123), then list your name and social security number on Schedule C of your 1040 tax return (where you'll report your income and business expenses) and you'll be all set! You aren't required to use your name in your email address, website or phone number, but if you are undecided about the magnitude of your INCOME-MENTS, you can start by branding your name or something catchy that will cause people to think about YOU; because even if you don't know where all of this will end up, it's always a good idea to brand YOU.

Let's be clear: I'm not suggesting that you pretend to be in business, but rather, that you actually make a decision to BE in business for yourself and get educated about the tax benefits. Many homebased businesses do not require a license or a Tax ID number when operating as a sole proprietorship, but you should check with your local government for registration or permit requirements just to be safe. Now I'm sure you

41

understand that you cannot run a medical facility from your house: you would need a degree, a license, malpractice insurance, etc! I'm not talking about high risk businesses with licensing, board, and education requirements. When I say *"let the INCOME-MENTS begin"* and *"start your homebased business / sole proprietorship now,"* I'm specifically referring to a low-risk homebased business where you're operating as a consultant or independent contractor.

Let's also be clear about this: in order for your business to be recognized as a business and not a hobby by the IRS, you are not REQUIRED to earn a profit in the first few years, but you must have the INTENT to make a profit (you can have a loss for a few years) and you must run your business like a business by keeping good records. I use the Taxbot Software created by my mentor Sandy Botkin (get it at www.lynnrichardson.com). It tracks everything, including mileage from one location to the next using the information in my google calendar. If you don't want to use software, then do it the old-fashioned way and keep a tax diary: use a small spiral notebook or purchase my budgeting journal (it's a deductible business expense!) and write everything. When you pay for anything, anywhere, at any time, ALWAYS get a receipt, then write on the back: who was involved, what was the business reason, what you discussed (if it was a dinner meeting), where this took place, how much you spent (because receipts fade) and when the event took place. You don't need a receipt for expenses under $75 (unless it's for a hotel room) but I suggest you keep them all anyway. Record your daily business expense notes and mileage/driving details as if your life depends on it, because your wealth certainly does! And of course, meet with your tax professional to discuss all of your tax options and how they impact you personally. Or better yet, join TaxBot University online and take the same classes I did, led by my mentor Sandy Botkin (this is a miniscule investment in yourself, it is also a deductible business expense and it can be found at www.lynnrichardson.com).

NEWSFLASH: Your accountant can't tell you EVERYTHING you need to do to properly document and deduct your business expenses, so don't start beating up on them! The tax code is entirely too broad for your CPA/accountant to teach you everything you need to know. Most people are shocked when I tell them about hiring their children in their homebased businesses and the first thing they say is, *"My accountant never told me!"* It's not your accountant's job to do that. It's literally a gamechanger for you financially; it's your job to learn and apply what you learn if you want to **get _your_ money back**. Some say this is hard work, but so is being broke! It takes a lot of mental energy to spend your time robbing Peter to pay Paul, so choose to do THIS work and remember my mantra: ***it's always business and* everyone's an entrepreneur.**

So . . . did you think starting your business would be more complicated than this? You might be thinking, *"I need a business plan,"* or *"I need direction,"* and you are right. Sure you will need a business plan to grow and sustain your business (I will share a few valuable nuggets a bit later), but you don't need a business plan to start a low-overhead, low-risk homebased business / sole proprietorship. I don't want you overthinking and under-executing this step. Just do it! Before you know it, your business will actually grow as a result of your effort; you will be self-motivated – or should I say **"get-your-**

money-back-motivated" — to keep ethically sound and impeccable business records; you will interact with more business people who think like us; AND you will **get your money back** during tax season! Now doesn't that make dollars AND sense?

Yes?

I thought so!

Now, let's get you out of the wilderness . . .

Take a look at your talents, skills, and other opportunities so you can transform them into INCOME-MENTS.

LYNN'S EXAMPLE:
List one talent, skill, or opportunity that could generate more income.
I can teach people how to create and balance multiple streams of income and how to run their businesses and document their expenses properly so they can save money on their taxes.

How can you use what you wrote above to create an income stream?
1. *I can write a book and sell it online, in local bookstores, and throughout social media.*
2. *I can do speaking engagements.*
3. *I can teach online classes.*
4. *I can teach other people how to teach other people. I can have a train the trainer program.*

Write three things you will do in the next 30 days to implement this income stream:
1. *I will write, edit and print the book.*
2. *I will submit it to Amazon and my online store.*
3. *I will tell the world about it through social media memes, videos, and passing out flyers everywhere I go.*

Now, it's your turn!

Create the 1st INCOME-MENT in Your Symphony:

List one talent, skill, or opportunity that could generate more income.

_____

_____

_____

How can you use what you wrote above to create an income stream?

_____

_____

_____

_____

_____

Write three things you will do in the next 30 days to implement this income stream:

_____

_____

_____

_____

Take a look at your talents, skills, and other opportunities so you can transform them into INCOME-MENTS.

LYNN'S EXAMPLE:
List one talent, skill, or opportunity that could generate more income.
I can teach people how to create and balance multiple streams of income and how to run their businesses and document their expenses properly so they can save money on their taxes.

How can you use what you wrote above to create an income stream?
1. *I can write a book and sell it online, in local bookstores, and throughout social media.*
2. *I can do speaking engagements.*
3. *I can teach online classes.*
4. *I can teach other people how to teach other people. I can have a train the trainer program.*

Write three things you will do in the next 30 days to implement this income stream:
1. *I will write, edit and print the book.*
2. *I will submit it to Amazon and my online store.*
3. *I will tell the world about it through social media memes, videos, and passing out flyers everywhere I go.*

Now, it's your turn!

Create the 1st INCOME-MENT in Your Symphony:

List one talent, skill, or opportunity that could generate more income.

_____

_____

_____

How can you use what you wrote above to create an income stream?

_____

_____

_____

_____

_____

Write three things you will do in the next 30 days to implement this income stream:

_____

_____

_____

Create the 2nd INCOME-MENT in Your Symphony:

List one talent, skill, or opportunity that could generate more income.

_____

_____

_____

How can you use what you wrote above to create an income stream?

_____

_____

_____

_____

_____

Write three things you will do in the next 30 days to implement this income stream:

_____

_____

_____

_____

Create the 3rd INCOME-MENT in Your Symphony:

List one talent, skill, or opportunity that could generate more income.

_____

_____

_____

How can you use what you wrote above to create an income stream?

_____

_____

_____

_____

_____

Write three things you will do in the next 30 days to implement this income stream:

_____

_____

_____

_____

Create the 4th INCOME-MENT in Your Symphony:

List one talent, skill, or opportunity that could generate more income.

_____

_____

_____

How can you use what you wrote above to create an income stream?

_____

_____

_____

_____

_____

Write three things you will do in the next 30 days to implement this income stream:

_____

_____

_____

_____

Create the 5th INCOME-MENT in Your Symphony:

List one talent, skill, or opportunity that could generate more income.

_____

_____

_____

How can you use what you wrote above to create an income stream?

_____

_____

_____

_____

_____

Write three things you will do in the next 30 days to implement this income stream:

_____

_____

_____

_____

Create the 6ᵗʰ INCOME-MENT in Your Symphony:
List one talent, skill, or opportunity that could generate more income.

_____

_____

_____

How can you use what you wrote above to create an income stream?

_____

_____

_____

_____

_____

Write three things you will do in the next 30 days to implement this income stream:

_____

_____

_____

_____

Create the 7th INCOME-MENT in Your Symphony:

List one talent, skill, or opportunity that could generate more income.

_____

_____

_____

How can you use what you wrote above to create an income stream?

_____

_____

_____

_____

_____

Write three things you will do in the next 30 days to implement this income stream:

_____

_____

_____

_____

Create the 8th INCOME-MENT in Your Symphony:
List one talent, skill, or opportunity that could generate more income.

_____

_____

_____

How can you use what you wrote above to create an income stream?

_____

_____

_____

_____

_____

Write three things you will do in the next 30 days to implement this income stream:

_____

_____

_____

_____

Create the 9th INCOME-MENT in Your Symphony:
List one talent, skill, or opportunity that could generate more income.

_____

_____

_____

How can you use what you wrote above to create an income stream?

_____

_____

_____

_____

_____

Write three things you will do in the next 30 days to implement this income stream:

_____

_____

_____

_____

Hire Employees to WORK the INCOME-MENTS in Your Symphony: How much do you spend annually on your child, grandchild, niece, nephew, God-child or other relative? (this is just a sample list, not comprehensive)

Gifts (birthdays, graduations, Christmas, etc):

_____

_____

Vacations (summer vacation, spring break, reunions):

_____

_____

Extracurricular Activities (fees, uniforms, events, games, competitions, etc):

_____

_____

Tuition (academic, dance, karate, special classes):

_____

_____

You cannot write anything on this list off! However, if you hire the person and pay him/her a salary or fee, you can deduct this as a business expense on Schedule C of your 1040 tax return. The person STILL gets what you were going to give them anyway, but now, you can **get your money back** during tax season!

What can the people above do to WORK the INCOME-MENTS in your business and earn an income?

Who can model?

Who can do social media?

Who help with chores in the home/home office?

Who can do bookkeeping? (recording expenses)

Who can do administrative functions?

Who can help at events?

What other jobs and candidates can you think of?

The Hybrid:
Employee / Business Owner

Now, let's talk about how you can **get your money back** if you are an employee at someone else's business AND you have your own business. What I'm going to share does NOT work if you are simply an employee. You will owe the IRS. This will work if and only if you are a hybrid: Employee/Business Owner.

If you are currently operating under the first system as an employee, then you receive a paycheck every two weeks, every week or every month. Whenever it is, chances are that your net pay is much less than your gross pay. When you were hired, the payroll department gave you a bunch of papers to complete. One of the documents you completed is called a W-4. If you claim one exemption on your tax return, then you probably claimed one allowance on your W-4. If you claim two exemptions on your tax return, then you probably claimed two allowances on your W-4.

Right?

Wrong! You are probably giving the IRS too much money when you get paid because you fear that you will owe money to the IRS at the end of the year. That fear is real if you do not have a homebased business, but if you do in fact start your homebased business NOW, you can avoid this. Even the IRS tells you to give them less money (IRS Publication 919). And if you get a tax refund, that doesn't make it any better. You are essentially giving the government an interest-free loan when you could use that money to fund your financial legacy or stop **Living Check to Monday.** Every time I hear someone who says, *"I got a large tax refund,"* but they're struggling to pay bills every day, I think *"Nooooooo! That's not the way to do it!"*

So what should you do?   I'm glad you asked! LOL.   Google the W-4 calculator on the internet and choose the option connected to www.irs.gov.   Read the worksheet and follow the instructions.   Contact your Payroll Department and adjust the allowances on your W-4. It's as simple as that.

Let me give you a real-life situation. I remember anticipating my very first bi-weekly commission check over $20,000 many years ago.   I had plans for this money, okay?   I figured after Uncle Sam took his part, that I would get around $16,000 since I had 5 allowances (I never read the form and I was doing this out of habit, like most people who are not knowledgeable about the real money game that is being mastered by the wealthy). But when I got that check, it was less than $12,000!!!! I almost passed out!   I think my staff almost called the ambulance.   But I needed my money so I couldn't pass out! Laughing but totally serious! Instead, I went to my office – I was running a branch as a very successful mortgage professional back then – and I called the IRS. When I tell this story, people often ask, *"What made you call the IRS?"* Let me tell you. I called the IRS because they are the people who had my money, and I wanted to know where my money was and I wanted them to give it back! LOL! I was connected to a withholding agent (I didn't know such a person existed) and I told her my situation. I said, *"I got this check. It was supposed to be $20,000, but you guys took out too much money and it's less than $12,000. This has to be a mistake."* She asked me a few questions, did her calculation, and came up with essentially the same number (it was two pennies off), and she explained that because I was earning large commissions, that I was in fourteen or fifteen different tax brackets that I had never even heard of! *"What?!"*

From that day forward, I knew I had to increase the allowances on my W-4. I got more money back on my next paycheck and I never forgot this lesson: wealthy people don't necessarily get more money, but they certainly know how to keep more, and if they spend it, they know how to get it back!

Later, I learned that I could pay my children to work in my homebased speaking business (they helped me prepare to teach classes at expos, seminars, etc). In addition, I learned many other ways to **get my money back,** so even though I increased my allowances, I had enough documentable business expenses to deduct on Schedule C of my 1040 tax return, so I didn't owe the IRS at the end of the year.

I'm eternally grateful that my God-mother told me to start learning from Sandy Botkin. Her situation was similar to mine. She was a Chicago Public School teacher making a very large salary. But her paycheck was pitiful. And to top it off, she owed the IRS at the end of every year and she was ALWAYS doing business on the side. Like me, she changed her W-4, she got $2,000 more on her paycheck every two weeks, AND she got a refund at the end of the year! THAT'S A LOT OF MONEY! So if you're a high income earner and you're still broke, take heed.

Now let me be clear: my God-mother keeps IMMACULATE RECORDS. She documents every single personal and business expense at the end of each day while she sits in her car before she enters her home in the evenings. I've watched her do it. That was too much for me; I'm not that disciplined! Instead, I wrote important details on the back of my receipts as soon as I received them from the cashier or checkout desk at the hotel, then I would put them all in my business expense envelope for that month, and finally, I would add everything to my spreadsheet at the end of the week or month. Now, I use the Taxbot software (www.lynnrichardson.com) on my mobile phone, I scan my receipts, I record them as personal or business, and at the end of the year, a nice spreadsheet is ready! Do whatever works for you, but the important thing is this: do something. Don't stay broke because you're too lazy to do the work and please don't give the IRS more money than you have to.

Get Your Side Hustle Game On!

Don't Quit Your Main Job! . . . But let me get this out of the way: yes, I did in fact quit my corporate job, but I struggled for a loooong time! I'm just telling the truth. I don't regret my decision because there were many factors involved (the economy crashed, my 401k AND my new opportunities dried up for a short time, I'm not a quitter, I had a plan and it was working, etc.). I was ready to live out my dream of helping celebrities and entertainers build their empires and it was the best decision for ME. If you are not ready to take the risky leap that I took, I think it makes sense to keep or find a job you enjoying doing as an employee (and get health, retirement and other benefits) AND get additional side jobs that can fit into your role as a consultant in your homebased business. One of couples I counseled on national television paid off $100,000 in debt in a year leveraging internal corporate opportunities, consulting work in their professions, and other retail / non-skilled jobs AND they kept their corporate jobs! Continue to be excellent on your main job; that's your first priority. There's no integrity in giving any of your jobs less than your best, simply because you have a new gig or a more exciting opportunity. I live by the golden rule of entrepreneurship: ***treat your employer's business as you would want your employees to treat your business***.

Now that we've gotten that out of the way, here are a few ideas to step up your side hustle game:

1. Look for extra shifts or additional commission-based opportunities within your company.

2. Start consulting using your natural gifts and talents (skilled based areas):

- ✓ teachers can tutor
- ✓ singers can perform at weddings and other events
- ✓ counselors can help families in the neighborhood, church, community center, etc.
- ✓ journalists can help bloggers with their writing or make public relations connections
- ✓ Human Resources professionals can help with resumes, interviewing, etc.

✓ attorneys can teach classes at high schools, colleges, community centers, etc.

3. Get other side hustles to simply bring in the cash you need (not based on any specialized education, skill or talent, but these could be cash cows nonetheless):

✓ Uber / Lift / Chauferring (especially if you own a really nice vehicle that will now be deductible as a business expense)

✓ Retail (Walmart, Starbucks, McDonalds, etc.)

✓ Home Care / Landscaping / Cut grass / Cleaning

✓ After Hours Clubs (security, bartending, etc.)

✓ Ushers at Festivals / Concerts

✓ Babysitting

✓ Pet care (petsitting, grooming, etc.)

✓ Car Washing (markets, sporting events, etc.)

With this exhaustive list of side hustles, now would be a good time to create a few more INCOME-MENTS in the exercise in the previous chapter. In addition, since we are talking about side hustles, I want to share the **Corporate H.U.S.S.L.E.** and how it works as contributed by my colleague Ingrid Lavon Woolfolk, a former Controller who served in corporate America for over 20 years, built her side hustle game with integrity, then transitioned full time to her own **H.U.S.S.L.E.**:

What exactly is H.U.S.S.L.E.? In urban neighborhoods, the word "hustle" (traditionally spelled) means to go beyond and take what's yours. Sometimes it means to take what has been promised, but not given. In life, you won't always be given what you desire, or are worth. But you can take it by creating something from nothing and offering it to those that find value in it. But are you prepared to H.U.S.S.L.E? Were you born to take what wasn't given to you? Are you willing to just "get by" until you can "level up?" In 2013, I decided to bet on myself. But I was smart, and I took it slow, created a plan, worked the plan, and created small wins that I would be able to string together to create bigger wins that would ultimately allow me to launch out on my own. I knew that I could live my dream while creating the ultimate life I wanted to live. Wouldn't it be great to wake with a smile, being thankful for simply waking up, grateful for having employment, create the best experience possible during your day, while coming home and building a company that would leave a legacy for your family? This may sound farfetched, but it can happen. While many of us have felt the confinement to our office space or cubicles, running your own thing isn't for the faint at heart. My grandmother always told me, there are Indians and there are Chiefs. Both are valuable, but you have to decide which one you'll be.

I was fortunate enough that in my 20 year Corporate career as Finance Executive managing anywhere from three hundred million dollars to one billion dollars in revenue over a 5 year period, I was able to truly make a difference. Whether it was leading an event for a caucus group, volunteering for a special project, or simply over delivering on the expectations of my role, sometimes it made me feel really good. But there were also stretches of years where I felt lost, and generally unhappy with both my personal life and my professional life. Many of us hide behind our titles. That was me. Our life consists of running from meeting to meeting and event to event. If we're not in the car, we're on the phone. My son would often say to me, "Mom—another event?" We love saying we're busy, but wouldn't it be nice when someone asks what you've been up to and you can say without hesitation, building a legacy! Imagine a successful business before the business plan is even created. Imagine writing a check to yourself and being able to cash it because the money is there. Being intentional about what you hear, who you're around, and where you go are critical pieces to this new journey.

*The true **H.U.S.S.L.E.** (**H**oly & **U**napologetically **S**tarting to **S**eek **L**iberation through **E**ntrepreneurship) requires the **Triple P Effect**: Preparation, Patience, and Prayer. Life is full of choices. Some are as simple as what you will have for breakfast or how much cash to pull from the ATM. Others will require much more thought and investment. These decisions are the ones that can either keep you stuck, or propel you into the next phase of your life. Preparation is the first step to identifying and understanding if you're willing and ready to make a transition out of corporate: financially and physically.*

Are you prepared to believe in your own success? Honestly, I was not. While I knew I was good, darn good at what I did, I relied on the name of the company to carry more weight than my own. When I introduced myself, the first thing I'd say was my name and who I worked for. This gave me a sense of validation and belonging. In a tough economy it is wise to sit with a financial planner and understand the implications of your short- and long-term plans, especially if you've been with the company for ten or more years. You have stock options, etc. that may need to be considered. You will also need to look at reducing any ancillary spending on items, foregoing a few getaways, and minimizing your splurging until you have a handle on the exact investment of both time and money that will be needed.

The physical aspect of preparation can be even more taxing than the financial piece. You may need to create a workout plan or simply increase your activity to provide an outlet for stress. There will be some stressful moments, and having an outlet to release some of the pressure will keep you sane. Preparing for this journey won't be easy, but it will be worth it if you stick with it, remain committed, and stay consistent in your actions.

Patience is one of those things that I have never really been good at. And in this societal climate, everyone appears to be getting successful overnight and making money moves. But no one seems to show the downside of the hustle. Someone once told me, to have patience is to have peace. The Bible speaks about patience frequently throughout both the old and new testaments. So clearly, it's important. However, many of us fall short. You will need a great measure of fortitude to endure this life changing experience. It won't come easy, and it won't come fast. However, with patience, things will begin to manifest only in a way that it could naturally happen. Do you remember when you met that perfect guy or girl and you just knew they were the one for you? And then your Grandmother would burst your bubble and say, "baby, just keep living, every leopard will eventually show his spots." This very saying would take the wind right out of my sail. But I knew exactly what she was saying. It was meant for me to take it slow, watch for the signs, allow things to happen without the use of coercion, and yet be intentional about the encounters and make every connection count. That's what you have to do when starting a business; be intentional and make every connection count. In my business today, my sales cycle is running about 5-7 months. When I'm introduced to someone that may need my services, it typically takes that amount of time for them to realize they need me and I want to work with them. Now some are sooner or later, but the average time is just about five months. This is enough time to complete due diligence, observe on both sides, gather the facts, and make wise fact-based decisions. You cannot expect nor do you want everything to happen in seconds. A successful, sustainable business is not built overnight. Be patient with the process and more importantly be patient with yourself and it will all work together for your good.

Prayer is the final, yet most important element of the H.U.S.S.L.E. Without much prayer and meditation, I would have gone back to corporate by now. Truth be told, I've tried a couple times and it simply wasn't in the plan. Again, I was impatient, and God was saying wait, I'm not done yet. My goal was always to leave Corporate America at 40 years old, but I wanted to leave on my terms. But having lived through 6 layoffs, wondering, and waiting for your name to be called or your phone to ring, I guess that was leaving on my terms. When it's time for you to move, you will be pushed. My prayers became stronger as the staff and people I had grown to respect and love dwindled down to just a handful. My prayer was that my family would be protected, and there would be minimal financial impacts if my name was called. Praying gave me peace, but it also gave me strength. I found the energy and the passion to work when everyone in my house was sleeping. Ideas and thoughts were given to me in dreams and all I would have to do is wake up and execute. I truly believe God heard my prayers because many of the things I asked for and wrote came to fruition. I wrote the number of clients I needed to exceed my salary; it happened. I wrote the amount of money I wanted to make on a monthly basis, and it happened. I even documented the days of the week I didn't want to work, and by God that happened also.

Each time I wrote, I prayed. Then I got to work. See, you can't pray and then lay back. You have to pray then work like your life depends on it, because it actually does. You could still be working your day job, but you know your life will be forever changed when that passion kicks in and starts creating the monetary rewards you desire to have.

Incorporating the Triple P Effect into your plan of entrepreneurship lays the foundation on purpose with purpose. You will begin to feel more comfortable with the thought of change and during your seasons of discomfort. The Corporate H.U.S.S.L.E requires you to have a beast-like mentality – a feast or famine mindset. You will create the level of endurance to push past the pressure and realize the fruits of all the sacrifice. When you're a hustler, you make a way out of no way. You create circumstances and scenarios others will either fail to see or second guess. And that's ok. This journey is not for the faint at heart. It's for those who can see beyond their current vision, and allow their actions, determination, and work ethic to take them to places they only imagined and prayed for. I am a corporate HUSSLER and you can be too! You can Live After 9 to 5, simply by following key business and no non-sense steps that will ultimately become your second career.

That's the H.U.S.S.L.E.!

Ingrid Lavon Woolfolk
Celebrity CFO, Profit Strategist, Author &
Curator of the "Living After Series"
<u>www.livingafterdivorce2.com</u> IG: @IamIngridLavon

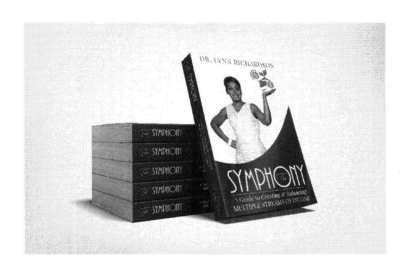

Live On Purpose!

Focusing your life solely on making a buck shows a certain poverty of ambition. It asks too little of yourself. Because it's only when you hitch your wagon to something larger than yourself that you realize your true potential. **President Barack Obama**

If you're trying to find yourself – if you're trying to discover your purpose – I'm advising you to do what I did: look in the mirror and let go. Do what you love with excellence and the money will follow. That's my motto. I stopped trying to discover my purpose and I simply began to live what I loved. Do you love to help people? Then perhaps you can live out your purpose as a teacher, a motivational speaker, a life coach, a therapist, or a counselor. Maybe you'll end up in some kind of service industry where you are using your gifts to improve someone else's life.

Are you very analytical? Do you enjoy details? Do you like sitting in silence solving problems that seem difficult to others?   Perhaps you will live out your purpose as an engineer, mathematician, chief operating officer, air traffic controller, mechanic, television producer or executive assistant.

I went from being a jack of all trades and a master of none to embracing who I am and what I love doing at the core: teaching. I started teaching people how to get approved for mortgages, then I would teach other loan professionals how to become successful, then I would teach the masses during each television and radio appearance, and as you read this book, I'm teaching you now. I love teaching and I've accepted that. As a matter of fact, it's almost impossible for me NOT to teach when I see an error, which invariably gets on everyone's nerves around me! But when I tell them, *"Okay, I won't say anything,"* then they all say *"No, we need you!"* LOL! And if that isn't enough, I can teach almost any meaningful life skill that will elevate the lives of others; hence, that's the core INCOME-MENT in my business symphony: teaching.

So instead of looking for your purpose, I challenge you to accept who you are and live on purpose, and as a result, those activities will give birth to the INCOME-MENTS in your business symphony. When you live on purpose, you embrace your values, you embrace your gifts, you embrace your skills and you even embrace your failures, because your failures taught you what NOT to do.

So how do you live on purpose? I'm glad you asked! Part One: Ask God to use you for the specific purpose for which He made you – without any involvement from your overthinking mind – then let go and let Him show you the way, so you won't have to worry about what you have to do or try to figure out how to use the gifts He gave you. When I was in my early 20's, as shared previously, it felt like I had 90 jobs! I eventually got tired of myself, LOL, so I just gave up and asked God to use me for what He made me to do. He knows me better than I know myself! Period. Look at this example: let's presume God inspired someone to make a fork for a specific purpose. When someone is eating steak, she will find a fork, not a spoon. The fork doesn't have to be anxious about getting picked. The fork doesn't have to worry about the "competition" (because the spoon is no competition at all!). The fork doesn't have to pretend to be something it's not. The fork just needs to keep being a fork and look like a fork and stay ready to be used when needed (the fork should not start moonlighting as a toothpick!).

I applied this theory to myself. God made me for a specific purpose: to teach. When someone needs a teacher (in business, finances, life, marriage, career, staying sane amidst life's hardships, etc.), that person will come and get me. I don't have to compete with anyone. I don't have to get anxious; I just need to consistently teach and look like a teacher and avoid trying to act like something I'm not: a singer (in case you didn't know, I canNOT sing!). When I made my first appearance on the Steve Harvey syndicated TV show, I knew I could do two things: (1) teach him and everyone in the building something they did not know about money, and (2) make them laugh while doing so, which lightened the load of the tough financial lessons I dished out. At the end of my segment, Mr. Harvey did not shake my hand. Instead, he approached me and said, "You're getting your own segment." Then he called his entire staff to the stage at that very moment, and the rest is history. The show needed a witty financial expert who could teach; so they came and got me. You were made for a specific purpose, and if you let God use you for what He made you for, when someone needs you, that person or company or group will come and find you. The universe will support your belief about who you are!

Part Two: Once you accept navigational direction in your life, remember that you are a servant, because it's easy to get a big head on your way up the ladder of success. Whether you are a CEO or a cashier, your job is to use what you have been given to serve other human beings. Perhaps you are good with fixing cars. Then you can give to others buy fixing their cars and by supplying job opportunities to those who can help you fix even more cars. When I was a Vice President at a Fortune 100 company, my head was BIG. I was cocky and arrogant. But at church, I was required to serve the ministers their dinner after service; they were not interested in my teaching skills clouded by bossy arrogance and untruth (I was secretly **Living Check to Monday** at the time, but I was unraveling very quickly). When I raised my hand to volunteer, serving food was NOT what I had in mind! Monday through Friday I was number one in corporate America, but on Sundays, I was a waitress and I wasn't even getting paid! And to top it all off, everyone who knows me knows this: I hate manual labor! I'm lazy and I will sit down the first chance I get! But I stuck with it for two years and I was eventually promoted to be in charge of the greeters. This posture of humility and servitude saved my life. I learned to be excellent, to keep my mouth shut (a nearly impossible feat), and to serve with excellence no matter the circumstances.

Part Three: once you accept navigational direction in your life and remind yourself daily that you are a servant, then you need to stay away from crazy people! I know, you probably were NOT expecting that. Here's the point: you cannot fulfill your purpose alone, so you must be surrounded by people who will support the direction and path for your life and business. No matter how long you have known someone (those childhood friends, family members, and college buddies, etc.), pay close attention to who they are and do not discriminate when it comes to cutting people off! If they are not right for your business, love them by leaving them right where they are so they, too, can live in their purpose and so you can keep it moving. When people show you who they are, BELIEVE THEM. People can lie but energy cannot, and the discerning part of you knows how to put two and two together. And if you've been hurt in your past, learn your lesson and let it go! Accept your responsibility in the situation and do better next time. I went through the most horrible relationship of a lifetime when I was in my late teens, but it did not stop me from receiving the love I deserved from the man of my dreams. My first assistant in the mortgage business was EXCELLENT at working but TERRIBLE at showing up! But it did not stop me from stating my expectations and trusting new employees later on. It takes teamwork to make your dream work and even though you will still have challenges with the people around you, say NO to haters, blockers, cheaters, liars, and users and be the best you can be so you can attract the best in others.

LIVE ON PURPOSE!

The Personality of an Entrepreneur

At this point, you know why it absolutely makes dollars AND sense to be in business for yourself, even if and especially if you love your current job where you participate as an employee (you don't have to choose; you can do both with excellence!). You are ready to get your side hustle in full gear and you are ready to live on purpose so you can develop the INCOME-MENTS in your business symphony. All is well, right? Wrong! You have a big issue that you need to resolve: understanding and executing the many personalities of an entrepreneur so your businesses will actually make money consistently.

THE DREAMER: When I went into the mortgage business in the 90's, it was my dream to become one of the nation's top mortgage and real estate professionals and to make a lot of money doing so. I was new in the business attending a company sales rally where people were walking across stage getting top producer awards, and as the announcer was calling out their stats *("Jane Doe, number one in the eastern region, did five million dollars in production")*, I was adding up their paychecks as they walked across the stage! I was sitting next to my branch manager who was also a top producer and because the buzz was already out that I was a dynamite rookie, I looked at her and said, "I dream that one day, I'll be on that stage . . . I hope." She continued to look straight ahead at the stage and said, *"Don't just dream, make it a plan. Hope is not a strategy."*

Ouch and Amen!

The first personality of an entrepreneur is the dreamer and the dream is the heartbeat of the vision.

Without the dream, the entrepreneur dies. I was on tour with my boss Russell Simmons during his Super Rich book tour on the west coast, and someone asked him, *"Russell, what do you do when one of your businesses fails?"* I was braced and ready for a BIG answer. Something profound. Instead, he said, *"You can't fail until you quit."* The end. I was floored! It was so simple, yet so large. That's the dreamer and the dreamer's job is to see the vision and to keep going. Don't quit.

THE THINKER: The thinker is the personality of the entrepreneur that will put a plan in place to make the dream a reality. The thinker knows that hope is not a strategy. The thinker is also the personality of the entrepreneur that will re-route the plan if the current plan is not meeting expectations. There's a distinct difference between the two: the dreamer will say, *"Let's keep going because we can't fail until we quit,"* and the thinker will say, *"If we keep going in this direction, we're going to fall off of a cliff and die, so we need to reroute!"* Without the dreamer, the entrepreneur dies, but without the thinker, the dream may never become a reality. The thinker is the strategic planner and a strategic planner is always asking questions: How is this dream going to come into fruition? Who do we need on our team? What do we need to know that we don't know? Who should we be in partnership with?

When I quit my corporate job, I was the top ranking executive in my division; I was the golden girl. I had taken an initiative that had only produced three million dollars over a three-year period to thirty-six million dollars in my first nine months. I just blew it off the map. When I left, I prayed for two things: I prayed for wisdom because I wanted to know what to do in any given moment and I prayed for discernment because I wanted to know who I should be doing it with. Wisdom is knowing what you don't know, and being vulnerable enough to get the help that you need. It's not trying to be a Wonder Woman or Superman, on the contrary, it's knowing this: *"Hey, there's somebody out there who's better than me in this particular area."* Instead of being worried that they're going to steal your idea, you should collaborate and learn from others when possible! The truth is this: if somebody else takes your idea, and doesn't do the right thing with it, it probably won't work and you still have a chance to bring it to fruition. If it does work, there are legal steps you can take: the alleged co-creators of Facebook received A LOT of money after Mark Zuckerberg made Facebook a virtual phenomenon. I believe the settlement was over sixty-five million dollars. I don't know about you, but after I got over my tears and anger, I think I'd be happy with sixty five million dollars for an idea I created that I would probably have earned far less on with my limited vision and knowledge. I'm not saying you should be careless with your intellectual property and give your ideas away; but I am asserting that you should discern who you should talk to about getting the help you need to make your business grow. In other words, don't be so afraid of other people stealing your ideas that you won't even sit down with an attorney to help you protect them!

THE STORYTELLER: The marketing personality of the entrepreneur shows up in the storyteller. The storyteller is the one who invokes excitement in others about the dream and who articulates the internal and external plan for accomplishing the dream. The storyteller will ensure that everyone within physical and virtual reach will know about the INCOME-MENT in question and will even help spread the word about your business symphony as your vision materializes; hence, the storyteller is responsible for expanding the brand.

THE HUNTER: The hunter preys on new business opportunities without ceasing. The hunter understands that in the world of business, you will thrive in a feast or die in a famine, and the hunter is consistently looking at multiple ways to bring income into the business. When I started in the mortgage business, I learned very quickly that everything I did was about the hunt. After I closed my first loan and made over two thousand dollars, I decided to hire an assistant to take care of the faxing, photocopying, message answering, etc., so I could focus on my highest and best use: hunting and teaching. I created homebuyer classes so I could teach attendees how to become homeowners. I taught at churches and schools so people would choose me to help them build wealth. I went on the radio to teach financial literacy and eventually my phone was ringing off the hook. (This is where the thinker comes in to develop a plan to manage growth). I was constantly on the prowl for referrals from real estate and other financial professionals whose values were in alignment with mine and no matter how much money I made, I never stopped hunting. One of my favorite books about business is **The E Myth** by Michael Gerber. In it, he describes the entrepreneur who thinks vision and passion and skill are enough to sustain a business, but who quickly learns that the business crumbles without people who plan, people who handle the small things, people who tell the story every day and in every way possible, and most importantly, people who consistently focus on bringing home the bacon.

The key to building consistent INCOME-MENTS in your business symphony is to understand how to balance the multiple personalities of the entrepreneur. You can't just dream and if all you do is think, you may never execute. If you hunt without the help of a thinker who develops a viable plan, you may waste time, money and other valuable resources like your sanity! I was so busy working so hard and hunting impulsively, that I would burn myself out every ninety days. That's no way to exist and it's not sustainable. Finally, the goal is for your business to get bigger than YOU and if no one tells the story, others won't be able to help you hunt nor will they ever be in a position to hunt for you so you can create passive income. Once you're earning passive income, money you don't have to work for, you will be well on your way to balancing a beautiful Symphony . . . Now go get'em!

Essential Resources

<u>Books</u>
7 Simple Ways to Legally Avoid Paying Taxes

Save Money on Your Taxes: Big Time!

475 Tax Deductions for Businesses and Self-Employed Individuals

The "E" Myth: Why Most Small Businesses Don't Work and What to Do About It

<u>Government Resources</u>
https://www.irs.gov/newsroom/hobby-or-business-irs-offers-tips-to-decide

https://www.sba.gov/blogs/5-reasons-hire-your-child

IRS Publication 15
IRS Publication 334
IRS Publication 465
IRS Publication 535
IRS Publication 919

<u>Other</u>
Lynn Richardson's Chores Checklist to Help Any Parent Get Their Kids on the Right Track!
Email: management@lynnrichardson.com

Everything You Want to Know About TaxBot, TaxBot University, and Sandy Botkin
www.lynnrichardson.com

Join the Movement:
www.hiphopsistersnetwork.org

About Hip-Hop Sisters Foundation
Co-founded by Lynn Richardson, Felicia Shaw, and MC Lyte, the legendary lyricist and iconic hip-hop pioneer, **Hip Hop Sisters Foundation** is a non-profit organization that promotes positive images of women of ethnic diversity, bringing leaders from the world of Hip Hop, the entertainment industry, and the corporate world.

HHSF provides national and international support to women and youth around the globe on the topics of:

Cultural Issues; Financial Empowerment; Health and Wellness; Mentorship; and Educational Opportunities.

Celebrity advisory board members include Faith Evans, Ledisi, Jada Pinkett Smith, Russell Simmons, Cheryl "Salt" James, Malinda Williams, Malcolm Jamal Warner, and Dr. Benjamin Chavis.

Hip Hop Sisters Network welcomes and embraces partnership opportunities with individuals and institutions that contribute to the empowerment of people across the globe.

About Dr. Lynn Richardson Lauded by the masses and named by Urban Influence Magazine as one of the 20 Hottest Influencers in America, *Dr. Lynn Richardson, also known as the Madea of Money,* is an ordained minister, television and radio personality, author, tv/film executive producer, entertainment executive, life coach and financial expert who uses her quick wit and humorous presentation style to help others face their money issues and achieve personal, professional and spiritual harmony. With more than two decades of leading roles in the financial services industries, Lynn's vision of helping others financially has become a global reality. Lynn has served as Chief of Operations for Russell Simmons' and Dr. Benjamin Chavis' Hip Hop Summit Action Network, and is currently the President and CEO of MC Lyte's Hip Hop Sisters Foundation, and President and COO of MC Lyte's Sunni Gyrl entertainment and celebrity management firm, where she oversees entertainment and empowerment strategies that impact the globe.

Lynn is the host of the syndicated daily radio show, **The Millionaire's Roundtable,** where she is committed to *Creating Millionaires One Family At A Time.* Follow **@LynnMillionaire** on social media. **Get help and listen live from anywhere:** www.LynnMillionaire.com.